3D COACHING

3D COACHING

Suggestions for a New Approach

MICHAEL A. BROWN SR.

Right Fit Communications LLC

Contents

Dedication vi

INTRODUCTION

1. 5-Step Process to Success 6
2. 3D Principle 15
3. Why Do I Coach? 21
4. Where Do I Begin? 29
5. What Kind of Coach Am I? 40
6. EI Can Help You 60
7. Self Preservation is Key 65
8. The Total Coach 69

References 76

About The Author 77

Dedicated to family, friends, and faith, which allowed me to share my experiences. Shared in honor of all the coaches who came before me and all those who will follow me.

Thanks to Curfew Speight and all the athletes like him who played for and with me and who became remarkable men and women. I cherish you and I salute you.

Thanks to my copy editor, Chandler West, for another great collaboration.

Copyright © 2021 by Michael Brown

All rights reserved. No part of this book may be reproduced in any manner whatsoever without written permission except in the case of brief quotations embodied in critical articles and reviews.

First Printing, 2021

Introduction

"Leadership is based on inspiration, not domination; on cooperation, not intimidation."
  William Arthur Ward
  American author

I have played football, baseball, softball, and basketball for many years at many levels. What I am most proud of is that I got into coaching before my 22nd birthday, many years ago. I went to watch to a practice where my friend's brother was playing. They told me they needed a coach and asked if I had some time. I said yes. It was the best thing I ever did! Some days I felt like I did not know what I was doing, but the kids and I learned from each other and we worked it out.
Looking back, I realize the good things I did and the bad things I did. At that time, I learned that just because you play a sport does not mean you can coach it. I also learned that not all skills come naturally to all people. When that is the case, it is necessary to understand how to teach the skill so that a player can master it.
Vince Lombardi said, *"Coaches who can outline plays on a blackboard are a dime a dozen. The ones who win get inside their player and motivate."*
Since that early coaching opportunity, I have tried to follow Lombardi's advice. I have coached various sports in recreation leagues, military leagues, men's and women's leagues at the local level, high school leagues, and middle school leagues. I was a player on some of those teams, a player-coach on others, and

just a coach on others. My experiences gave me a chance to look at coaching from both the player's and the coach's view, often at the same time. These were amazing learning experiences that enriched me and clarified my outlook on football coaching in particular and on sports coaching in general.

Those great memories led me to merge all my time and experience into a coaching philosophy that can work for any coach in any sport. I offer my techniques and suggestions to new coaches or to coaches who want to reenergize their coaching interest or approach. However, even the most experienced coach might be interested in a different approach to the challenge of motivating women and men to victory in sports and in life.

I learned a lot during my time as a player and a coach over the years, but my greatest lessons came when I served in the Air Force for 24 years. Military service has so many of the same characteristics, especially in leadership, as coaching does. You are trying to get several people from different walks of life with different skill sets to come together to achieve a common goal. There is competitive stress in both, just in different ways. In coaching, you are challenged by the enormous responsibility of managing the care and development of others (often someone's child) while exposing them to heavy competition, a chance of injury, and the stress associated with success and failure.

In the military, you are doing all that and more, oftentimes with a danger component in some austere part of the world. Many of the people you lead are away from home and their families for the first time in their lives. You must teach and protect at the same time. So, in reality, the foundation of my coaching philosophy comes from my military service. This book is my attempt to share my thoughts about leading people whether the environmental pressures are high or low. Both coaching and military service require you to be your best and give your best to those you coach or lead. Let me share that with you.

My coaching philosophy is *3D: Dedication, Detail, Discipline*. I refined this over the last 10 or so years of coaching, and I now use it with the staffs and players I am involved with at every opportunity. Not everyone will see the value in this approach, but I will explain it to you. Let's take a close look at the words in 3D.

Dedication

ded·i·ca·tion /dedəˈkāSH(ə)n/: *Noun*: the quality of being dedicated or committed to a task or purpose.

Coaching Note: Success has a price. That price is dedication to the task at hand through hard work. That price is being determined to do the best you can, win or lose. That price is applying the best of yourself to everything you do.

We must teach players to be dedicated to working out alone and with the team to get in the best shape possible. As coaches, we need to study our craft and search for ways to teach skills to players of all ages, motivating along the way.

Detail

de·tail /dəˈtāl,ˈdētāl/ *Noun:* an individual feature, fact, or item.

Coaching Note: Paying attention to detail means demonstrating to your team, and yourself, that it is necessary to focus on the journey, not just today's goal. Learning the right way to compete is vital to having the confidence to grow as a person and as a team member. The leader's job is to create the perfect conditions for success by teaching techniques and strategy. Once that is accomplished your team can use their talents and their wits to grow and win.

We must take the time to learn each player so we can understand their motivations and their challenges, allowing us to help them focus their strengths and improve their weaknesses. Coaches need to be good listeners and dedicated teachers to demonstrate the skills required of our team so that we can do the little things right. Success in little things leads to success in big things.

Discipline
dis·ci·pline /ˈdisəplən/ *Noun:* to train or develop by instruction and exercise, especially in self-control.

Coaching Note: Discipline is important all the time, but it takes on more importance when things go wrong. You cannot change what happens, but your discipline provides you with the tools to change your approach, your attitude, and/or your response. Discipline guides your ability to avoid complaining in troubled times and instead working with your team to figure out how to make things better.

We need to teach student athletes to pay attention to the rules and to be the best they can at home, in school, and in the sports arena, in that order. Coaches need to set and follow the same high standards to be effective role models. We need to understand that the players are always watching and, if we are successful, will follow the lead of the coaches.

New View of Success
This book offers a new view of success in coaching that is not tied to any sport. This approach is about knowing yourself and your team and developing together to form a winning combi-

nation that can withstand the test of time. This approach is based on getting the best out of players and coaches together through a common language and a shared understanding of the formula for success.

Each chapter, including this introduction, offers you a system or guide to help you find your way and stay on course to be true to your vision and achieve your team and personal goals. My 5-step approach for success is (1) Learn, (2) Look in the Mirror, (3) Know Your Team, (4) Win the Race, and (5) Enjoy Yourself. This is the approach that will help you instill 3D as the culture of your team.

I have given 3D and the 5-step approach a lot of thought. I have worked through the pros and cons as a head coach and an assistant coach. I have compared this approach to the approaches of coaches I worked under, searching for the plusses and minuses of their approaches versus my thoughts. In this book, I want to reach out to those who are looking for help in their coaching approach. When I went to a certain school to coach the Wing T offense, I needed to know more about how it was run. I purchased a book written by a national guru of the offense and then went the extra step to meet him at a clinic. One of our coaches and I treated him to dinner, and he talked us all the way through the system. That helped me immensely. I hope I can help someone else in a similar way.

Chapter 1

5-Step Process to Success

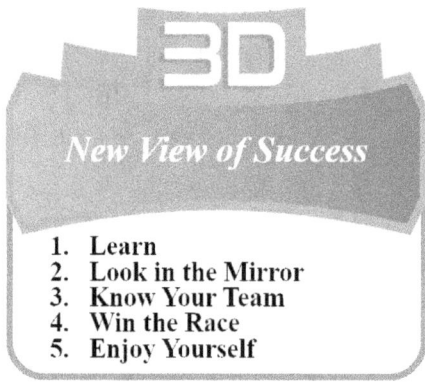

Figure 1. This process is about continuous learning, self-examination, team building, effort, and having fun.

Learn About Success

"Tell me and I forget, teach me and I may remember, involve me and I learn."
  Benjamin Franklin,
  Founding father

When I developed the 3D principle, I quickly realized that it needed to be accompanied by a solid process. I developed the 5-Step Process of learning your craft, looking in the mirror, knowing your team, winning the race, and enjoying yourself. I designed this process from those plusses and minuses I discovered when I was that 22-year-old new coach, and I refined the process with all the experiences I have had since. By sharing precise steps to guide your efforts, I hope to give you a formula you can follow as long as you coach.

When using my process, start with learning your craft completely by going to coaching clinics, reviewing videotapes, reading books, and talking to other coaches. Work on upgrading your skills and observe how successful programs operate.

Coaching clinics expose you to new ideas and give you a chance to have deep discussions with other coaches. They also feature the latest in technology to help you with your coaching activities. Watching videos is important because you can slow down and dissect the action to examine every detail. In fact, many coaches tape their games and watch videos with their players. You must find your preferred way of reviewing film and then select the right segments to share with your players and coaching staff. No coach can know everything there is to know.

Networking and exposing an open mind to new ways of doing things can be helpful in one of two ways. One, it can give you the answers to problems or issues you are dealing with on your team. Two, it can verify that your approach is a good way or the best way to proceed. Or you might find out a little of both.

Look in the Mirror to See Success

"Character cannot be developed in ease and quiet. Only through experience of trial and suffering can the soul be strengthened, ambition inspired, and success achieved."
  Helen Keller
  American author

Second, take a good, hard look at yourself and your program. Analyze your program's strong and weak points. Look for ways to enhance your strengths and improve on weaknesses. Find out how successful programs handle issues and concerns like those in your program. Examine how well your team emulates your behavior and what you believe in.

Good coaches evaluate themselves all the time. Great coaches take an in-depth look after each season to determine the plusses and minuses of how things unfolded. Even a championship coach can make the team better, guarding against complacency and reduced effort. These can happen if the coach or the team members convince themselves that their status as champions it a guarantee for the coming season.

You can also check with other successful coaches and teams to get a look at their formula for success. As yourself if any of the things they do can help your program. Most of all, examine your team culture and make sure you continue to grow those values in the hearts and minds of your staff and players.

This type of self-assessment is part of increasing something call metacognition, which is improving the process you use to plan, monitor, and assess your own understanding and performance. Metacognition offers the benefits of understanding how your brain works so you can determine the best approach to learning. What you find out will help you avoid or approach learning tasks, thereby allowing you to improve weaknesses and maximize strengths. This learning should also allow you to work through processes that effectively lead to increased long-term performance and retention.[1]

Know Your Team to Pursue Success

"Coming together is a beginning. Keeping together is progress. Working together is success."
   Henry Ford
   American auto maker

"If you want to lift yourself up, lift up someone else."
   Booker T. Washington
   American educator

Third, know your team. What do you want for your team and how will you make it come to pass? Who are your players and what do you owe them? Do not forget your parents and supporters and their importance to a team and family atmosphere.

Compare your goals for the team to the individual goals of the players, especially any new players you have. The new players need to adjust to the culture, and the best way to help them is to find out what they see as success and relate that to your team values. Make sure they know that there are ways for both team and personal achievement to exist.

Make sure the members of your team know you are invested in their improvement. Be proactive by giving regular, constructive feedback as you go through drills. Practice this same approach in games, stressing positive actions and results even when you are losing. Feedback is especially powerful when it is unexpected, positive, and informal. If you can make this a regular ongoing dialogue with your team, you will have a great tool for motivating them. If you connect informal feedback with the knowledge you gain about your players' goals and wishes, you will improve your communication power immensely.

Show each member of the team that you value their participation by talking to them and listening to what they say. This fosters a sense of belonging that is so important to building a great team. Share your success stories with your players. I like to expose my players to people who have played for me in the past. I don't organize formal speeches. I just let former players know they are welcome at my practices and I let the team know who they are. The actual conversation is up to them. I am just creating the atmosphere for information sharing.

Coming up with unique rewards is another way to build your team. We have seen some college teams use a lunch box for hard workers, while others use chains, hats, or other props to reward the player after a turnover. The great thing is that the rest of the team celebrates too.

Give everyone a chance to be involved by introducing flexibility in your practices. Sometimes I have selected the best drill to teach something, but once we get started, I find that some players are uncomfortable because the drill might require a skill that is a problem for them. I must pay attention and either change the drill or get through it and introduce a "balancing" drill, so everyone has a chance to succeed in a drill.

Another good approach is creating innovation space where players can test their skills. Sometimes it is good to split the team into smaller groups and have competitions, such as an obstacle course. This allows them to try out new skills and allows you a chance to look for hidden talents. Take advantage of what you learn! Make sure that these types of approaches are not the exception. They can help you on a regular basis.

Also understand that with players and fans, you may be leading a community. If your culture and your values are understood, it will give you opportunities for successful interactions with parents and other family members outside of the team. Finally, understand the stressors that may affect your players and talk about them. Your players will appreciate these approaches, even if they do not tell you.

Win the Race to Success

"Our greatest weakness lies in giving up. The most certain way to succeed is always to try one more time."
    Thomas Edison
    American inventor

Fourth, consider yourself a runner in a 100-yard race. Run to win. Do not let anyone work harder than you do and never let your team down. If the team needs something done and no one is doing it, adjust your strategy to put someone in charge or restructure your approach to make the team successful.

As much as I hate to say this, it is not necessary to win every time, but never lose because of lack of effort or failure to adapt to a new situation. Set challenging, realistic goals. An example of that would be running your 100-yard race as if it is a 110-yard race. That guarantees you a level of effort that will challenge and motivate your entire organization. Hard work is contagious.

That kind of high goal setting will challenge you and force you to work harder to succeed. The extra effort resulting from high goals may show that you have capabilities beyond the limits you imagined. Stretching yourself in this way builds character, stamina, resolve, and many other positive traits.

Help your players understand the benefits of effort. People may have varying skill sets that influence their success or failure in completing tasks. Tell your players that they are totally in control of their effort regardless of their skill level. Continuous effort can deliver successful results.

The tough part about extra effort is that you may not be able to coach it into players. They must be ready and willing to give extra effort. You will find that if they believe in your culture or if they simply want to perform at a higher level, they will give that extra effort.

As I said, you may not be able to coach extra effort into your players, but there is one thing that I have found helps bring it out in your players: competition. Create competition in your practices and you will find those players who give the extra effort. They want a starting position. They want more playing time. They want to be the best on the team. They want to be named captain. All of these promote extra effort by creating competition.

Enjoy Yourself on the Journey to Success

"Don't judge each day by the harvest you reap, but by the seeds that you plant."
  Robert Louis Stevenson
  Scottish novelist

Fifth and most important is to enjoy yourself. Coaching can bring overwhelming joy and satisfaction, even when your team is not winning. People appreciate teams and organizations that run efficiently and with a sense of purpose, but they really enjoy teams that are having fun!

I have been on successful teams that failed in the playoffs or in the championship game. The loss was difficult. Just as difficult was trying to find the positive aspects of the season when it had just ended. I remember struggling to remember the great days along the way to the end of the season.

In contrast, I have been on less successful teams that lost in the first round of the playoffs or, in some cases, did not make the playoffs at all. We remembered that every day it was a joy to be part of those teams. We looked back on so many good days and we retained the friendships years after playing our last game together.

Let me share an example of what I am talking about. This happened when I was coaching a recreation league team that lost to the league champions every year.

One year, we approached a mid-season game with the defending champions. The players decided on their own to gather earlier than normal, and they were more ready than ever to play. It started raining and I was afraid we would not be able to play, so I shared that with the players. They said they were ready to play no matter the weather. With our enthusiasm at an all-time high, the other team decided they did not want to play in the rain. The decision was made to postpone the game, which we lost in a close contest. My team was more confident than ever after that, despite losing to that team in the championship game.

The bottom line is that we had fun and we did more with that team in those years than we ever thought possible. Those players and some of the cheerleaders are still connected with each other and with me. We keep reliving the memories of that fun, rollercoaster season. Amazingly, I coached that team in the early 90s.

So please, learn your craft and honestly evaluate your program. Know your team and nurture their wants and needs to build a cohesive unit. Win the race by setting your sights past the finish line and running farther than you need to. Above all, have fun and enjoy yourself and make sure everyone around you does the same.

Now that we have a foundation for success, I will introduce my 3D principle of coaching.

Chapter 2

3D Principle

Figure 2. Your team agrees to commit to be dedicated, focus on vital details, and honor discipline in all things.

    I teach a 3D principle, which is Dedication, Detail, and Discipline: Dedication to the team, a focus on attention to detail, and discipline at all times.

    It all starts with the first D, which is about being dedicated to your team and to the task at hand. The second D is about paying attention to detail to make sure you do all the things required of you and making sure that you do each task correctly. The third D refers to discipline in all things, from family to school to team rules to personal accountability. Use 3D to teach your players and to make sure they are learning good techniques and sportsmanship.

Dedication

The first D, Dedication, signals what we believe. It forces us to look inside ourselves and determine what we believe in. Our fundamental beliefs about life and love and faith are particularly important because those are the things that guide our lives. If we dedicate ourselves to something that goes against those values, we end up in a constant struggle. This is key for the team dynamic.

There must be a fit between our personal values and the team values if we are to be successful. We face challenges and decisions every day, and our values help us work through those things. If the team fits your values, you can make decisions on the fly and be successful in competing as part of the team. When there is a good fit, you easily participate in the things the team wants you to do. You can pursue your personal goals and team goals simultaneously because of this fit. This does not mean that there will not be times when you and the team struggle to get on the same page, but a good fit minimizes those issues.

However, if there is a disconnect between your personal values and the team, there is a chance coaches will be in constant stress. Coaches may have difficulty making the decisions required to compete as part of the team. This kind of conflict can be counterproductive for the coach and for the team. This can create a struggle to do the things the team needs because they may go against personal values. Even if a coach accepts the team's position, that choice can cause increasing coaching stress over time because of the conflict I mentioned.

There are certainly times when conflict is good. For instance, when there is a new coach or a change in team, there will be an adjustment period as the coach learns the team's values and fits them to personal values and expectations. This is a healthy transition time if coaches can align their values sufficiently once they understand the team values.

Always keep in mind that achieving the "good fit" may not last forever. Changes in players and coaches and administrative aspects of the team present a challenge in finding an acceptable balance between your values and those of the team. Still, Dedication requires commitment to giving heart and soul in pursuit of achieving and maintaining that balance.

Detail

Detail is the work "where the rubber meets the road." Attention to detail is all about honing your skills and perfecting your craft. We all must be open to learning new things and developing our current skills. We cannot be satisfied with today's performance, even if today brought a championship or some other personal achievement.

Many people say success is a never-ending journey. If you become satisfied with what you have accomplished lately, you will struggle to muster the focus and effort to work as hard tomorrow as you did yesterday. That hard work is what keeps you on top, or at least keeps you striving for the top.

Always strive for accuracy in all things. As you perform, you will confront risks to your success. I am not only talking about your risks. For you and the players these risks could include failing to manage the day's events and being late to practice, forgetting the game script or socks or a mouthpiece or a jersey on the way to a game, or even players avoiding telling the coach they do not know the plays they are required to know. These are risks and you should identify, analyze, and quantify them so you can work to eliminate them.

For the late practice, set up your schedule the night before by detailing everything you need to get done before you go to practice. Help the players work out the same preparations. When players have a problem with forgotten items, help them develop a game or even a daily checklist of the items you need for the game and put them all in one place where they will not forget.

For the difficulty learning plays, have open lines of communication. Make sure you know the plays and that your staff knows the plays. Then make sure the players know there is no penalty in letting the coaching staff know early that they are having problems. Maybe you and the staff can work with a player who is having a problem or can put them together with another player or players who can help them learn.

Practice is also about Detail. Work towards a state of perfection by identifying the tasks needed to succeed and working through them methodically. Use repetition to make task accomplishment a habit. Try to create game situations whenever possible to demonstrate the speed, stress, and challenge of actual games.

Detail requires diligence and communication through effective listening skills. Take all the time that is required to achieve the desired outcomes. Keep in mind that preparation, planning, and design are the keys to setting up practices that matter and that move you and your team toward improved performance.

Listen to your players about what they are experiencing as they learn and practice their skills. Allow players to question what is going and to suggest ways they want to approach things that are difficult for them. You do not always have to agree with them, but you have to listen. You will be surprised at how much your players appreciate it when you listen to them. Listen to them even when you do not think it is related to the task at hand, because they may be reaching out to you about an issue they are struggling with. This will build trust in players and they will not be afraid to come to you if they have a problem.

Discipline

There are three types of discipline: preventative, supportive, and corrective. Preventative discipline explains the actions taken before an undesirable behavior to stop it from happening. Supportive discipline explains the actions taken to help a person reshape or redirect their own behavior. Corrective discipline explains the actions taken as a consequence of undesirable behavior.

The previous discussion about Dedication and Detail provide methods that should guide team-friendly actions in the process taking care of preventative discipline. If successful, we can limit or eliminate undesirable behaviors and make corrective discipline unnecessary.

Discipline as used in 3D is supportive. Discipline moves coaches to work together with their players to discover their potential and set a course to continued success. Being supportive can take many forms. Coaches can change strategies or techniques to be sure they are capturing the attention and motivation of their players.

Coaches can also be supportive by showing interest in each players' life beyond the current season or sport by asking questions and making comments to foster good communication. Always use eye contact to show you are genuinely interested in the person, not just the athlete. When a player is struggling with a skill, use physical proximity to demonstrate your commitment to their improvement and to get them back on track.

Sometimes suggesting other ways to do a task can help players succeed. One other good approach is to give the player small challenges that they can manage on their own. For instance, ask the player if they would like to stay with the current drill while the team moves on, or ask the player if they would like to meet with you after practice and try again. Both of these approaches take the spotlight off of the player's struggle, at least for the moment.

Supportive Discipline encourages everyone to find what works best for them and pursue that answer. Allowing this kind of discipline may pull the team apart a little, but I assure you the team will be stronger when the player in question fixes the problem and rejoins the group effort.

Beliefs, values, challenges, decisions, competition, fit, conflict, adjustment, transition, alignment, commitment, balance, skills, learning, performance, achievement, accuracy, risk, preparation, communication, practice, perfection, demonstration, trust, behavior, supportive, potential, success, strategy, plan, and technique. These are the key words in our discussion of 3D coaching. They represent keys to success in coaching that results from healthy communication with your team, a shared understanding of the skills that lead to success, and a commitment to the behaviors that support individuals and the team equally.

My3D approach can be applied at any level and in any sport. As part of the strategy, for instance, I might work to get my players to talk about school at the end of each practice, making school a part of practice. A few years back, we had a current events day where each player had to come ready to tell us about a story they read in the paper or a magazine or heard on the news. I have often found ways to run study hall to help players who are having problems. I always ask, "What did you do in class today to support our football team?" If you keep education and sports in their proper place, your players will follow your lead and keep them in perspective.

Now, I want to focus on why I coach sports.

Chapter 3

Why Do I Coach?

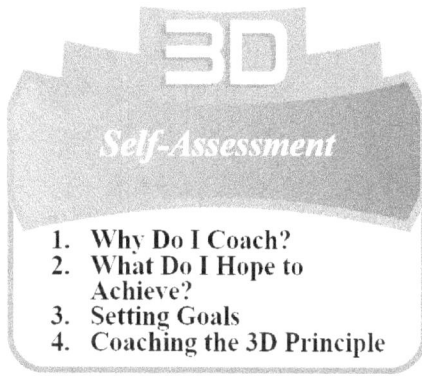

Figure 3. Understand your reasons for coaching and have clear goals that you will follow to success.

Why do I coach? What do I hope to achieve? These are the first questions you must answer when you begin working with athletes regardless of their age.

Many times, the first coaching opportunity comes without warning. Someone asks you to replace a coach who quit or was asked to leave. You may have gotten involved for other reasons. I have talked to many coaches who got involved because they were not satisfied with the way their son or daughter was being trained, treated, or mentored. Or maybe you are a coach just because you wanted to get involved.

Whatever your reason, you took the important and rewarding leap into a great volunteer activity and, maybe, a great profession somewhere down the road. There are never enough coaches for all the sports and athletes, so thanks for your contribution!

If you have not already done so, ask yourself two particularly important questions. I am not asking how you ended up in the position. My first question is **why** do you coach? Second, **what** do you hope to accomplish through coaching? Finding these answers should allow you to really sink your teeth into coaching. Maybe you asked these questions the last time you coached. Do not rely on old answers. Ask yourself again at the beginning of every season so you have a fresh understanding of, and focus on, why you are doing what you are doing.

The why is important because it provides motivation for the road ahead. The answer to this question can lead you to a vision that will help you achieve your goals; whether they are limited or comprehensive, short- or long-term, or are focused on championships or consistent success. That vision will motivate you in the tough times. Let me assure you that after more than 30 years of coaching various ages in various sports at various levels, I still encounter many challenges about how long I want to coach and what school or program can make me happy. Yes, there are many rewards and many exciting and enriching experiences, but there are also days when you wonder why you put up with this thing called coaching.

The challenging times are best managed based on the "what" question. If you know what you hope to achieve, you can adjust your efforts to suit that level of accomplishment. More important, you can set or reestablish goals and objectives that lead to success. It is also important to answer the why and what for your players.

Get your team involved early using questioning techniques that allow players to participate in goal setting. Team members can produce a consolidated, cohesive, inspired statement of the future they are committed to creating – constant improvement, undefeated, state champions, all stars, college scholarships. Athletes should have a vision that helps with their quest for personal meaning and accomplishment. Good coaches discover and try to consider each player's personal expressions of a dream as they relate to the team's goals. If they do not have a personal vision and goals, give them the time and encouragement to develop them.

What are your goals? Many coaches, athletes, and teams have goals that are directly tied to winning, so let's talk about winning. However, keep in mind that not every coach is in it solely to win championships. The harsh reality is that sometimes you do not win, but you can be successful even when you do not win. If your players improve, if you move your program to the next level, if you set yourself up for good things in the future, you are successful.

But back to winning. Winning is certainly a universal goal, but many coaches are more focused, at least initially, on teaching the basics and producing better players. I have listed some examples of high school goals below, and I am sure you can think of many more.

- Improve individual grade point average
- Improve team grade point average
- Undefeated
- Make playoffs
- Advance to regionals/semifinals
- Advance to state
- Win state
- Undefeated state champions
- Get student-athletes to college
- Showcase all-star caliber players

It is important to win, but ultimate success is a by-product of well-coached, disciplined, fundamentally sound teams. Yes, many times one team is simply more talented or better coached than another team. However, very often the fundamentally sound team can overcome better talent. I am talking about the kind of team that is created through a sensible approach to coaching that stands the test of time. Standing the test of time also means accepting failure from time to time. Here are examples of failing before winning.

- Michael Jordan was cut from his high school team. He went on to become the college player of the year, a national champion, an Olympic champion, an NBA champion, a scoring champion, defensive player of the year, and a regular season and playoffs most valuable player.
- Jordan returned from a largely unsuccessful pro baseball stint to win three consecutive NBA championships for the second time in his career, returning to his status as the best player in the game.
- The Denver Broncos lost in the Super Bowl four times before beating the Green Bay Packers in 1998.
- The New England Patriots have won six Super Bowls in 11 appearances.
- The Denver Broncos have won three championships but have lost the championship game five times.
- Some said the American Football League would never be as good as the National Football League, until the New York Jets beat the Baltimore Colts in 1969 and the Kansas City Chiefs dominated the Minnesota Vikings in 1970.
- The 1969 "Miracle Mets" that won the National League East title in baseball with a 100-62 record. This was the

first winning record in Mets history for a team that lost 101 games in the 1967 season.

What do I mean by standing the test of time? I mean that coaches who run these sensible systems pay attention to detail, stay consistent, and strive for continuous improvement. They are consistent in what they do. They set up a system, do what they do well, and keep looking for different ways to improve on their strengths. These coaches do not really change what they do. They improve the way they perform, and they find ways to make it appear to be something different.

Passing the test of time also requires that coaches improve and/or reinvent themselves whenever necessary. They go to coaching clinics, talk with successful coaches about how they get it done, and study films of successful techniques, programs, and players. They perform a hard self-examination by looking at their team on film and determining how they would beat themselves.

Great coaches constantly try to see their own weaknesses and work to improve them. All these things can equate to success over time. The greatest challenge to any coach is longevity, because you are only as good as your last team.

Great coaches also know that the players' continued growth is the primary requirement for success. What are you doing to help them? Are you stressing fundamentals, discipline, and accountability? Do you make education more important than sport?

In addition to paying attention to education, are your players getting the skills to be successful on the next level? It is important to know that you are preparing your players for the next level – whatever that may be. Whether they are off to some other team, some other sport, or just to the world of work, they are moving on to bigger and better things. What are you doing to help them cope?

Are your players getting noticed? Part of every coach's job is public relations, making sure that the people at the next level know who is on your team. Make sure you can give every player your personal recommendation and make the necessary adjustments in how you deal with that individual if there is a problem. You owe them a recommendation whether it is for the next level of sports or a job. They are giving you the best of themselves.

Whether your recommendation is to a college for academics or to a local business for employment, get them noticed. Getting them noticed includes doing interviews with the local paper or TV station. Journalists are always scouting for the star player's information, but you are the master of the quote. Be sure to take time to mention the unsung heroes. That mention may not always get aired on radio or TV or appear in print, but there is no chance it will see the light of day unless you say something. Work with reporters to talk up all your players, not just the stars.

While we are talking about taking care of players, be sure to ask yourself what they really want. Answering this question can help you shape your approach to leadership, motivation, and team building. There is no right answer, but there are some common things that people of all ages want.

Your athletes want a chance to play, improve, be challenged, and make a difference. They want to contribute in ways that count. They want to learn and master new skills. Yet, it does not stop there.

Your athletes want to be respected, trusted, supported, recognized, rewarded, and treated fairly. Most importantly, they want to own something, to have control over something in which they get to decide. They want freedom to act and react naturally so that they control the action.

Pay special attention to that need for ownership. If they are committed, they are not simply going along for the ride. They will work as hard as is necessary, even when you are not watching, because they feel they are working with you – not for you – to make the team successful.

So, the keys to your coaching challenge are understanding, developing, and ensuring longevity.

Your Coaching Challenge	
• Understand why you coach	Always make sure that you know why you are coaching. If you do not know, take time to find the answer or it may be time to leave coaching.
• Understand what you want to achieve	Determine the end state you are looking for in each season, just as you want players to do. Is it a championship, a winning season, or something tied to the individual successes of your athletes?
• Develop your players	Study your craft so that you can provide instruction in the form of drills that build skills and make the mastery of those skills something that will last over time. Make it second nature.
• Coach to stand the test of time	You will encounter many different personalities in terms of players, parents, and administrators. Can your approach build character that shows itself year in and year out? If your annual review keeps requiring you to make changes, go back and think about "why you coach."

Table 1. Keys to be successful in coaching.

How well you address these issues will determine the kind of coach you are. Your performance in these areas is the key to your coaching.

I am going to offer some ways you can handle the challenge ahead. They are things that work for me, and I hope they work for you. I am sharing my coaching trials and tribulations because the most important thing I have learned over the years is that you cannot get better by yourself. Coaches need all the help they can get. I know that sometimes it is hard to ask for help, but it is well worth the effort.

Let's get started!

Chapter 4

Where Do I Begin?

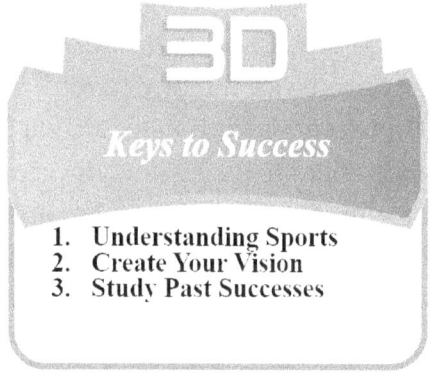

Figure 4. Analyze your sport and create a vision that allows you to be successful, modeling past success.

In our quest to use dedication, detail, and discipline, it is reasonable to ask where to begin changing or improving your skills to help your team. You want to understand the nature of sports and then create your own vision for success. A good way to future success is to study the past successes of yourself and others. This helps you to review challenges that have happened before and to analyze ways to use those past successes, or even failures, to help you in the future.

As discussed earlier, start by looking at yourself in the mirror. Revisit the reasons you decided to coach. Make sure you understand why you are coaching now, whether you are doing it for personal recognition, to help the players, to experience the glory of winning, to help the community, or to improve on what the last coach did to the team.

Knowing why you are in this thing called coaching is crucial to using self-examination leading to improvement. Remember, this is not an easy task. Coaching requires a lot of hours and a lot of hard work. In many cases there is no real recognition. In some cases, coaches are subjected to ridicule if they do not win or if they do not play the "right people." Some parents may be convinced they have superstars living in their houses, and some of them are correct. However, not everyone is a superstar, and you may have to be the one to expose the truth. You must handle both instances with care and diplomacy, so each athlete understands that she or he is your primary concern.

Even superstars must understand the importance of the team concept. More importantly, the team, family, friends, and fans must have a sense that each person has the same value and responsibilities to the goal.

Yes, you are charged with a great responsibility. Good coaching is about managing your players and the team based on understanding, vision, and reflection.

Understanding Sports

Now, let us examine what sports mean in our world. I will tell you what I think it is about, and then I will tell you what I think it takes to win – or to be successful. I make a distinction because I think you can be successful without always winning. Then, if you are consistently successful, you will win more than you lose.

Sports are about teaching fundamentals, motivating people to achieve a goal, rewarding 100-percent effort regardless of ability, and defining the role of athletic competition in society. Winning and losing usually take care of themselves. Talented teams can lose to less-talented ones because of the "fire in the belly" principle.

The "fire in the belly" principle says that if you are passionate about something and you put all your effort and ability into the preparation and execution of that something, you can succeed. In some instances, the fire just might be more important than the "something." You cannot expect successful endeavors without the fire. It is dangerous to just go through the motions.

You can see the fire in the belly principle in many of history's greatest sports upsets. I checked ESPN.com and they listed the top 10 greatest sports upsets of all time.

1. U.S. beats Soviets Olympic ice hockey, 1980
2. New York Jets defeat Baltimore Colts, Super Bowl III, 1969
3. Villanova tops Georgetown to win 1985 NCAA championship
4. Buster Douglas KOs Mike Tyson for heavyweight championship, 1990
5. Man O' War loses only race, to 100-to-1 shot upset, 1919
6. Denver Nuggets eliminate Seattle SuperSonics in 1994 NBA playoffs
7. Jack Fleck beats Ben Hogan at 1955 U.S. Open
8. New York Mets defeat Baltimore Orioles for 1969 World Series
9. Rulon Gardner overpowers Alexander Karelin for Greco-Roman wrestling gold, 2000
10. N.C. State knocks off Houston to win 1983 NCAA championship[2]

As you can see, these are 10 examples of days when one team or man is expected to easily win, but the underdogs with the fire in their bellies turned the tables. They were more prepared, more determined, more focused, and more intense than their opponents. Who knows the real reason? It does not matter. These 10 winners dreamed big dreams and won the big game.

Yes, there are many days when someone does not prepare for competition, or does not work hard in competition, or is not ready to sacrifice for the goal of the competition. On those days, any team or any athlete can win. If all things are equal in the competition, the team or athlete with a fire burning in their belly will be the engine that wins the race.

Even when you do not win the race, you may simply get a moral victory that will help you later in the season, in your career, or in life. The real win is the unconditional effort you bring to the contest.

For instance, in the late 1980s I coached a new basketball team of 10- to 12-year-old players. I was feeling important because we were regular-season champions, and I was the all-star team coach. This was not a team of all stars. It was a dedicated, hard-working team. The next year, the military moved me to another base. Once I got settled, I took on a team with much less talent than my previous one, but this was a group of young men who desperately wanted to learn the game.

I shared with them right up front that we would make up for any talent we lacked by being the hardest working team in the league. So, we started by learning defense. We learned to pressure the ball, to trap ball handlers and make them give up the ball, and how to rebound. This was crucial because we had difficulty scoring.

Unfortunately, we did not win a game that season, but we held every team below their scoring average. In fact, we lost five games by less than 10 points combined, and we took one of the best teams in the league into overtime before losing by four points. We improved our scoring over the course of the season, and all my players stayed with the sport the next year. We learned how to work hard and despite the lack of wins, we had a very productive season.

That experience is in stark contrast to my previous championship basketball team, on which four players made the all-star team and we finished the season undefeated. We did not have playoffs that year, so we played an exhibition with a local all-star team, losing a close game.

Even on that championship team, we addressed challenges. While our first seven or eight players were particularly good, I wanted to develop the others. We worked hard, but we had one young man who had never played basketball before. Steve was 10 years old and small for his age. He could not dribble, and when he shot the basketball, he could not even reach the backboard.

I devised a personal training plan for Steve with the help of his parents. This was in line with my vision of wanting to be the best basketball team possible. Since he could not shoot the ball high enough to reach the rim, he could not do lay-ups or shoot free throws. Steve would come to practice and warm up with the team, then do push-ups while the other players went through their shooting warm up drills. He did 50-75 push-ups every day in practice because we wanted to improve his upper body strength. Then, he would stand under the goal and throw the ball up as high as he could against the backboard. He did this every day, and then joined the rest of the team in dribbling and defensive drills.

He started to get stronger as the season progressed, and he improved his ability to dribble. Steve was getting closer and closer to making a basket in every game, even though he played only a few minutes of each. The team set a goal that all players would score at least one basket in the season, but by the last game they were very worried. Our season had only one game left and this young man had not scored.

We built a lead in the second half of that game, but it was close – we were never ahead by more than five points. Steve went into the game several times but could not score. Finally, with about four minutes left and my team hanging on to a small lead, one of our stars came over and asked if he and two others could take turns sitting out to let Steve play and score a basket. I was concerned, but something made me say yes.

As you may have guessed, with just over a minute to play, Steve hit a jumper for two points in a game for the first time his life. We finally had a comfortable lead, but the players celebrated like he had hit the winning basket in the Olympics. They celebrated so much that we got a warning for delaying the game.

Steve's improvement in that season was not even our biggest victory. My favorite memory of this young man is that he continued to improve in the off-season, and the next year he was a starter for his next coach. He had learned how to reinvent himself and he had found confidence through sports. That was the real championship of that season.

The two basketball teams are examples of creating success, not of winning and losing. This is about the joy of competition. This is about determination. This is about belief in the team concept. Most of all, this is about making life better through sports.

In both instances, I knew why I was in this thing called coaching. Make sure you always know why you are involved in coaching. Any time you are not sure, stop, step back, and take a moment to find out. If you cannot find a reason and you cannot ignite and sustain the fire in your belly, it is time to move on.

If you do have that fire yet, you are ready to craft your vision.

Creating Your Vision

The best place to start is with a vision, or a star you can focus on. Your vision is the foundation on which you will build your current and future success in coaching. It entices you to follow a reasonable path in looking toward the future. It points to where you should go, where you must go, to find success. By working out your current and future objectives for coaching, you will be in great position to educate your players on the path to self-improvement and team success.

Your vision guides you. You should review and revise it as necessary, but if you give it the right amount of thought and consideration up front, only minor changes will be needed. The vision keeps you from getting stuck in the challenges of the day-to-day grind of coaching, keeping you moving along your decided path to success and helping you meet your long-term goals.

Beyond vision, it is especially important to balance individual and team needs and to ensure a stable environment. Balance is difficult to maintain in the confusion of daily activities, but it is important just the same. It is also important to nurture your players' personal needs, so they will keep their perspective, direction, and motivation.

How does a coach craft their vision? Where does it come from?

Vision comes from effective coaches continually examining the big picture and working to determine the best way to take advantage of what they see. They visualize where they want to go and convince their athletes that it is the right path. These leaders motivate everyone around them to go along for the ride on a journey that will bring success to everyone involved.

The coach's vision begins the team's collective reach for growth and challenge leading to a brighter future. It electrifies preparations and practice sessions and gets everyone's adrenaline flowing. It brings a promise of better days ahead. For instance, each year when National Football League training camps begin, every team envisions a trip to the Super Bowl. When teams in various sports begin preseason practice, every player at some point thinks about winning a championship. When high school football teams begin two-a-day practice in preparation for the upcoming season, teenagers fantasize about state championships. Those visions of the ultimate prize create an electric atmosphere.

Your job as a coach is to energize people to commit to the effort and to enthusiastically put the team's goals above their personal wants and desires. It is astounding that people can be ready, willing, and able to put even grievances aside when they are exposed to a vision that clearly maps out the kind of team they want to be part of. It is even more exciting when athletes see how team success can translate into satisfaction of personal goals.

My message to athletes is that if you take care of the team, the team will take care of you. Sharing this electricity, excitement, hope, and optimism creates a team on the move. This electrically charged atmosphere almost always improves efficiency, cohesiveness, and creativity, and can be amazingly easy to maintain. Supporting your vision with the right goals and actions to get the job done does just that.

The challenge for every coach is keeping sight of the vision when things go wrong. Your vision should keep you on that path to your success or destination by helping you make the right choices and adjustments. Staying the course in this way gives the team confidence that success is ahead.

The team needs a consolidated, cohesive, inspired statement of the future everyone is committed to create. Players use the team vision to guide their efforts and to illustrate the team's goals. Allow players to pursue their personal vision if that pursuit does not contradict or interfere with the team vision. If you have players who do not have personal visions, give them the time and encouragement to develop them.

Vision is easy to understand, but it is sometimes hard to convey the nature of the required commitment before setting goals and objectives. Sometimes, you can convey the nature, but your people may or may not be willing to continue to give the required level of commitment over time.

I experienced a perfect example of the waning commitment problem a few years ago when I coached a football team. The team had a vision of winning a state championship and the most outstanding players had personal visions of making all-star teams. Unfortunately, not everyone who *said* they were committed could keep focused on that commitment. It was hard for them to continue to do everything required to support the "state championship vision." The problem was that not everyone understood that while it is easy to say you are committed, it can be exceedingly difficult to keep a daily focus on that commitment. The other difficulty is continuously making the sacrifices required to ensure the team succeeds.

The team I mentioned had poor discipline, poor attendance, and little respect for team rules. Not everyone understood that while the vision supplies electricity, concrete actions are required to support the vision and keep the "current" alive. When players are late for practice, get in trouble in school, disobey a coach's instruction, or do not give 100 percent preparing for games, it has a negative effect on the team and moves you away from your vision. We had talent, but we lost more games than we won because not enough people were interested in putting the team's interests above their own. Not enough people accepted responsibility for the vision.

Additionally, not all players and coaches understood that taking care of team needs makes it easier to take care of individual needs. Once people commit to satisfying team needs first and sharing the responsibility for success, vision can take its proper place at center stage.

Sharing this electricity, excitement, hope, and optimism creates a team destined for success. It also supports the goals that every team has, like improving the team grade point average, having an undefeated season, getting players on all-star teams, getting players to the next level, or finishing in the top 5 or 10 in all statistical categories.

So, what kind of team do you want? When people hear the name of your team or come watch you play, what can they expect? What rewards can your players expect? Where do you want your team to be in terms of progress and knowledge of the game at season's end? How have you prepared your players who will return to your team next year?

A perfect example of vision was a team I coached at Langley Air Force Base in Hampton, Virginia in the early 1990s. They were 11- to 14-year-olds and they were good, but they were a middle-of-the-pack team that lost to a visiting team from Pittsburgh at the end of every season. The team would come into town for a tune-up game just before the playoffs.

I was informed that Langley never beat this team and, yes, in my first season, we lost again. The other coach came up to me after the game and said that we should come and visit them in the summer for an exhibition game. I accepted on the spot, without thinking about the financial implications.

Leading up to the next season, I told the parents and players that our vision was to be a top team, beat Pittsburgh twice and go to the championship game. They were not crazy about the idea, and they did not believe they could beat Pittsburgh once, let alone twice. I finally sold them on the idea that we could raise the money to go and that if the players put in the work, we could do it.

That team worked harder than almost any team I have ever coached. They used the electricity of our championship vision to get in shape and to master their fundamentals in every aspect of the game. They prepared so well that we went to Pittsburgh and beat them soundly, then overpowered them when they came for their November return match. We finished as the runners-up in the championship game of our league. And Langley never lost to that Pittsburgh team again because they declined to play us when we called for a fourth-year rematch.

All our Langley Eagles success started with a vision of better days ahead. Now that's electricity!

Chapter 5

What Kind of Coach Am I?

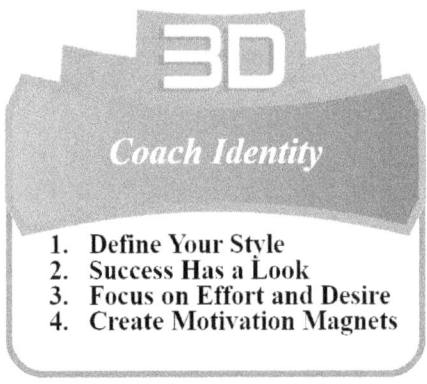

Figure 5. Use personal style and a vision of success, then use effort, desire, and motivation to achieve it.

As we talk coaching success, we need to focus on style, presence, motivation, and identification of or development of team leaders.

To do all that, you must decide early on what kind of coach you want to be and build on that decision. Some coaches pride themselves on winning. Some gauge their success on how many players they send to "the next level." Some are most interested in teaching the fundamentals so that every player knows how to play the game. Others are great motivators who can take any team with any talent level and be successful. Some coaches take a simple approach of making sure that every player gets a chance to play. I am sure you can think of a great coach who is a combination of all these things.

Define Your Style

Decide on the kind of coach you want to be and let that decision guide your efforts. Knowing what you want to be as a coach is valuable because it can give you energy when you have none left. It will help you find time when there is no time. The knowledge will get you through the tough times, when players, parents, or fans do not appreciate you. Most importantly, understanding the kind of coach you want to be will ensure that you pay attention to important considerations to make it all come together.

What am I talking about? This is about that first time your player says, "Coach, I understand" or "Coach, I did it."

I pride myself on being a motivator and a fundamentalist. My definition of a fundamentalist is a coach who breaks the game down into its simplest form and teaches the parts, then builds it back into a whole. I learned that from my football coach when I played in Germany from 1988 to 1991.

That coach artfully dissected offense, defense, and special teams into specific drills that developed specific talents. Offense day was a set of technique, speed, and agility drills that combined to represent precision and flexibility in running plays. Defense day focused on technique, strength, and aggressiveness to represent the power to impose our will on an opposing offense. He took the same approach to special teams. The result was a fast and exciting team that was motivated and successful.

I was the motivator when I coached teenage girls' softball in Germany. We were supposedly the second-best team at Sembach Air Base that year, and the previous year's champs had a great coach and some super athletes. We may not have been as talented, but our team had some incredibly determined young women.

The team was doing well, but we lost our first game to the defending champions. It was a close game, but we were intimidated by their previous successes. After the game, we talked about what happened and why we lost. The team had a players-only meeting after the game. Later they told me they had decided that their desire to win the game was not strong enough and that they were afraid to lose. In fact, they told me they expected to lose. I realized my motivation efforts leading up to the game were inadequate to develop their confidence.

Also, I tried to prepare them so that they would not make mistakes, and so that they would watch out for the other team's strengths. I did not spend enough time stressing our strengths. I did not let them know I wanted them to play the game as hard as they could *their way*, because I felt that would be enough to win. I did not share with them that I had great confidence in them. Coaches make this mistake often, not letting their players know how much they believe in them. This experience taught me to play to my team's strengths. It taught me to be impressed with what my own team can do, and not to rely solely on what a "better" team will allow me to do. I call it attack, adjust, and attack again.

The next time we played "the champs," it was for first place. We were determined that we would play our game and fight to win, not be careful not to lose. The game was close in the late innings, when Antoinette made a big play in the outfield, then hit a home run. We had a lead, and our pitcher Alison closed out the other team without allowing another run.

We built on that win when we went on to a local softball tournament against some very stiff competition. We won the tournament. Imagine that. The team that had no confidence finally had all the confidence.

In another instance, I was the fundamentalist coaching football. Clarence wanted very badly to play wide receiver; he was too small for any other position. The problem was that he had never been taught to catch a football. He worked at it during tryouts, but he did not improve much.

Since he was so determined, I gave him a drill to do at home. He simply had to toss the ball back and forth in his hands 10 or 15 times, then grab it and tuck it under his arm. Occasionally he would need to throw it up above his head then catch it and tuck it under his arm. My staff gave him some other drills to put emphasis on finding a grip on the ball, and then putting it safely away as soon as possible.

I told him to do the drills for 30 minutes to an hour every day *in addition to practice.* A couple of weeks later, the coaching staff noticed that Clarence was catching more footballs, and his parents noticed that he was seldom seen without the ball. Clarence had used the drills to teach himself. By the end of the season, he was a primary choice whenever we wanted to pass the ball because he had achieved consistency. I was ecstatic that the drills had given him the fundamentals to succeed.

As I said, Clarence was small. Early in my coaching career, I would have put him in the game and made sure the quarterback knew not to throw to him or I would have found ways to avoid playing him. However, by this time, I decided it is important that all the athletes get to play. It is the right thing to do to reward them for practicing and, in recreation league, they all pay the same fee to play. They deserve to play.

I started my coaching career as a win-at-all-costs coach, but I learned the hard way that winning is not everything. I learned that it is important to prepare each athlete for competition, and it is important to know that you can rely on them when injuries or unexpected absences eliminate your star players. It is even more important to let each player know that you trust them and that you will give them a chance to play when the game means something, not after you are hopelessly behind or incredibly ahead.

It was 1977 and I was coaching a football team in Goldsboro, N.C. We were one of the top three teams. We lost to the first-place team, and then we beat the second-place team. We had some rather good players, but we did not have a lot of depth. In fact, by the latter part of the season, we were down to 14 players and we had to play the undefeated first-place team again.

The week before that game was a bad one. One of our best players bruised his shoulder making a tackle the game before, so he could only play quarterback (the injury was to his non-throwing shoulder). Another player had to go out of town with his parents on an emergency. We went into the game with just 13 players.

The other team scored right away and was driving for a second score when we forced a fumble. We tied the game just after halftime. In the second half, their offense was more aggressive, and it was tough trying to hold them off. The team was getting tired because we did not have enough players to substitute. Remember that I had a player with a sore shoulder who could not play defense, only offense.

As the game progressed, one of my players, who took medication for hyperactivity, was ejected for biting another player. We were down to 12 players and their offense was still on the move. I turned to Danny, one of my youngest players, and told him to go in the game on defense. What he said crushed me. "Coach, it's not my turn to play," Danny said. "What do you mean?" I said. "I never play until the very end of the game, so it's too soon for me to go in," he said.

My heart sank, and I felt ashamed. I had given Danny the impression that I did not care about his contribution, that we did not need his participation. That may have been what I believed before, but now he was crucial to our continuing the game. I had failed as a coach. I had not prepared him. Desperate, I was able to convince him to just go in and do his best. Danny entered game and helped our defense hold and get the ball back. We scored a touchdown on our next possession and ended up winning the game.

I did not celebrate the win. I reminded myself that I had let Danny down. I realized I had let his parents down, and I had let the team down. I had also let myself down.

That is the day I promised to prepare every player to play, and to try to find ways to get everyone participation at meaningful times in the game. I never again want to put a player in the same position as young Danny.

As you approach your coaching career, always remember that you are a teacher. It is your job to teach young men and women how to play your sport. They cannot always grasp all the complexities of the game, but you must make sure they understand enough to compete. You must make sure they can participate without being embarrassed. That is your responsibility.

I understand that there will be times when athletes cannot compete. They may not grasp the basics. They may not work themselves into good enough shape in time to play or, sometimes, they really do not want to play the sport. Be honest with them. Let them know where their strengths and weaknesses are and let them know what you expect. If you are going to keep them on the team, decide how and when you are going to use them and explain their role. Make sure they understand and let them ask questions. Doing all of that will give them something to prepare for and give them a sense of belonging.

The hardest question I ever heard from a parent was posed to a coach who had been winning for years. In this season, she was losing games. The parent said, "I understood that my daughter wasn't good enough to help you win, but why isn't she good enough to help you lose?" The coach could not answer the question. My goal is to never be asked that question.

Sports are about involvement. Great coaches find ways to get everyone on the team involved. They find ways to teach fundamentals, allow participation, and win games. Even when they lose, they are winners because they are teachers. Never forget that.

The best thing you can do is find a perspective on winning, preparing athletes for the next level, teaching fundamentals, motivating, and ensuring participation that works for you. Explain it to your team members and their families. Above all, be consistent in following your philosophy.

Success Has a Look

If you can recognize success, even in its early stages, you can use that knowledge to be successful in your own program. Success has a look. If you watch closely, you will see success in family settings, in sports settings, in workplace settings, and in everyday events. Successful people do things in similar fashion.

Everyone needs to understand success and successful people. Success does not happen by accident. Successful people put themselves in a position to be productive and competent at what they do. Successful people in organizations ensure they do what it takes to satisfy the mission. Successful organizations provide the resources and professional atmosphere that allow their members to do what they do best.

In sports, success is putting the team before yourself, sometimes sacrificing individual needs for the greater good. One player will step back to allow a teammate to step up or may step forward when a teammate falls back. Success is giving.

Success is an unshakable commitment to the goal. I have seen families who want to go on a Hawaiian vacation give up trips to the movies and dinner, video rentals, designer clothes, and the newest musical release to make the dream a reality.

They are fine with missing a fancy dinner and eating soup and sandwiches at home because it is for the "team."

In sports, that unshakable commitment takes the form of lifting weights two weeks after your season ends in anticipation of your next season. It shows itself when student-athletes work ahead in classes so they can finish early and go to conditioning. It is evident when players hold off-season workouts without their coaches, displaying that championship attitude. In every instance, the athlete knows that whenever she or he takes a day off from preparation, a potential opponent is still working.

I believe in the will to succeed or influence another person, something that is displayed when you do not think you can move another inch, but you do it anyway. It is when a friend or a player is about to make a mistake and providing advice even if you are not sure they will listen. It is when you do not want to go to practice, but you go anyway.

The picture of success shows people doing the right thing when no one is looking. It shows people continuing to work on a project when everyone else is gone, because perfection takes time. It shows people doing the little things that may not be getting done, even though "it's not my job." These images offer a preview of things to come, and they are important because this kind of reliability is worth gold. If people can be this reliable when there is no pressure, then you can bet they will be solid as a rock when the heat gets turned up.

Success shows in coaches who realize that players and staff members must understand what is expected of them and what they can expect from those around them. Those coaches communicate the roles and responsibilities effectively and consistently. They ensure everyone knows what they can expect from the head coach.

Success is clear and consistent communications. It requires making sure every person has an ability to give feedback on team activities. It also requires free and easy access to coaches and administrators when there is a problem. Everyone needs to have a voice in good times and bad.

Now, I hope you understand what success looks like. Be careful, because even when you look successful, the proof of the effort may be a long way off. The hard part of being successful is sticking to a plan. Many people know what success looks like, and they know how to pursue success. They get discouraged when things do not go their way early and they abandon their plan looking for faster results. Sometimes, you are successful right away and you forget what it took to be successful, so your good fortune is short lived.

This is where you see teams falter all the time. They win championships and then cannot duplicate the success the next year. That is because they forget that the effort and sacrifices it took to be successful are the same as what it takes to remain successful. Also, the competition sees what you are doing and sets their sights on your team as the symbol of *their* success. Everyone wants to knock off the King of the Hill.

What is my point? Success comes in stages. Success takes time. Success abandons those who rest on their laurels. Success requires constant attention. Success requires discipline.

No matter what happens, keep achieving in pursuit of your goals. If you feel you have achieved all your goals, set new, tougher goals. Even if you win a championship right off the bat, that is just the first stage. Now you need to strive to be consistently successful. Even if you do not get to the top of the heap right away, you will see little wins and small gains if success is in your future.

The first high school team I coached only won four of 10 games. I was an assistant coach who wanted to do all I could to lead my position players, make them leaders of the team and, in turn, lead the team to success. We worked hard and everyone took pride in their new role. While we did not have a winning season, we had two players in the top 10 statistics in our district for much of the season, and at least two of the players went on to play in college. We worked together to achieve small stages in our quest for success, and it gave us something to build on the next year.

Encourage your players, and yourself, to dream big and pursue those dreams. Encourage your players to dream but help them understand that success does not happen overnight. Being patient and applying the extra effort mentioned before are good ways to handle adversity and challenge. Help players set their goals and empower them to dream and pursue success.

Always be willing to spend the time it takes to get it done. That time can vary based on your goals, your players, your resources, and your achievements. Success takes time, and that time is required all year round. It does not matter if you are an organization with daily goals or a sports team with a season that lasts a few months. The difference between winning and losing is preparation.

In high school sports, for instance, there is a designated start date for organized practice. Successful teams have an off-season weight training and conditioning program. Players work out together without the coach in anticipation of the first day of practice. What some coaches and players forget is that there are other requirements to get ready for a successful season. Ask yourself and your team if the players are working as hard in the classroom as they would in the gym or on the field. Do the players understand that poor grades can eliminate them and can end their team's season before it begins? You cannot contribute if you are not eligible to play.

Just as important, do your coaches and players understand the importance of proper conduct away from sports? When you are a coach or an athlete, all eyes are on you. Are you conducting yourself in an acceptable manner? Are you stretching the limits of public and social behavior acceptability because you are a sports figure? You should not be. Again, do not let anything knock you off the path to your goal: success. My rule of thumb is you should not do anything you would not want your mother and father to see you do.

Once you have won, it is human nature to take a break. Be cautious about resting and do not rest on your laurels, at least not too long. Make it a truly short rest if you need it. Your competition is studying how you succeeded even before you accept your trophy. They are trying to get a head start on knocking you off, and every day you rest is a day they get ahead of you. The bottom line here is never let anyone work harder than you do. Prepare every day as if you have never won anything. Understand that proving yourself through hard work every day can make you near invincible. Even when you are not invincible, you will look like you are to your opponents.

Pay attention to what brought you success and each day look at what you are doing and decide if it helps your quest for success. If it does not help with the end state, does it make you a better student, a better person, a better athlete, a better coach, or a better teammate? Success does not happen by accident, so be deliberate in your attempts to make it part of your life.

I cannot say enough about discipline. Discipline is the glue that binds teams together. Discipline wins and loses games. Good discipline follows you into the classroom and makes you work hard. Good discipline convinces people to work on off-season weight training and conditioning. Good discipline allows for total concentration on the game and the goal. Good discipline leads to total focus on the task at hand. Good discipline instills confidence that you can expect certain results every time because the actions and behaviors of people around you are consistent with the rules.

Poor discipline translates to a lack of effort and negative results in the classroom. Poor discipline leads to lackluster performance and attendance in off-season weight training and conditioning. Poor discipline deteriorates concentration and allows individual selfishness and lack of teamwork. Poor discipline equals no focus on required tasks. Poor discipline leads to lack of confidence in the team and individuals and produces inconsistent actions and behaviors.

This examination of success is not a complicated one. Success has a look, and you should examine that look and find the right path to your own success. Also, everyone must understand that success comes in stages and takes time. For those reasons, pay attention to your environment and responsibilities and use discipline to help you climb the mountain.

Keep all those things in mind and you can be as successful as anyone.

Focus on Motivation

The real challenge in coaching is to find out what makes your players tick. A good way to motivate players is to help them answer the question, "What's in it for me?" Motivation is about connecting your activities with the efforts and desires of your players.

There are some very straightforward ways to motivate. I recommend focusing on the things below to create an environment conducive to motivating your players.

- Highlight them: One-on-one interactions
- Understand them: Discuss personal desires
- Praise them: Honor positive outcomes
- Equip them: Provide success resources
- Focus them: Co-create a meaningful task
- Train them: Skill development
- Join with them: Involve your players
- Cherish them: Believe in your players

No one item is more important than the other. Look at this like a cake recipe, where every ingredient contributes equally to the taste of the finished product.

Highlight your players through effective and regular one-on-one interactions. These are important because they give the player a sense of personal importance. I cannot think of anyone who would not appreciate the chance to sit down with the leader and discuss the task at hand and future possibilities. With one-on-one interactions, you send a clear signal of the person's importance to you.

Another way to show the person's importance to you is to understand their personal motivation through discussions of their personal desires. This should happen on a regular basis, not just when you are in a one-on-one discussion. If the person's desire is not wildly in conflict with team policies and goals, you can reinforce them in team activities. Understanding a player's personal desires gives both of you an opportunity to examine them and align them with team culture and team goals. This is important to motivating people.

Praise your players when they reach a goal or distinguish themselves in some way. A Gallup study found that recognition and praise are significant motivators to get commitment based on the results from companies with the highest engagement levels. Individual productivity increases were found in employees who received praise on a regular basis. These employees were also more likely to stay with the organization and received higher loyalty and satisfaction scores from customers. The poll results suggest that praising someone once a week makes a difference.[3]

Make sure your players are ready to succeed by equipping them with the proper resources. Every team has an equipment bag for practice. Do not limit yourself to those items when you are teaching. When coaching football, I use a medicine ball to help with stance and start drills. Some coaches use large garbage cans to get more repetitions when aligning the defense to various formations. Do what you need to do to get the right prop for the right teaching effort. This is an especially important area because, as recreation league and middle school and high school coaches know, many of the things you need are not in the budget. Be creative!

Focus your players on the success challenge by partnering with them to find what works for each player. If a player is struggling at a position they are trying to win, partner with them to reevaluate their skills. In baseball, for instance, you may find a great athlete who you want to play in the outfield, but you may find that their arm is not strong enough to make the crucial throws. Maybe you can use that athletic ability at second base or first base, where the throws are shorter but require faster action-fueled decisions. This cooperation can deliver benefits to the player and the team.

Train the skills of the game to put your players in the best possible situations. Sometimes coaches get comfortable with great athletes who do almost everything effortlessly, but we can improve their skills. Sometimes coaches do not find the time to work with less talented players on their skill sets, but we can improve their skills. We must remember that we need both types of players to succeed, and they need each other. Training gets everyone going in the right direction to develop personal and team improvement.

Join with your players to create a culture of success. Emphasize positive thinking and work ethic as the foundations on which you will be your great team. It is easy to make all the decisions yourself, but you will find it helpful at times to let the team discuss it and resolve the issue. There will be times when an informal leader arises in your team. Let that player work their magic of bringing the team together and addressing important issues. You may even find that the informal leader will bring issues to you before you are aware that they exist. This is an unexpected benefit because it creates a higher level of communication leading to shared understanding in your team.

Cherish your players by believing in them. Your belief gives them the confidence to give their best effort every time. Your belief allows you to give them time to work through problems. Yes, you will step in if things are going wrong, but you will find a level of creativity and execution that you never imagined. If you find you cannot cherish them in this way, go back to the other motivation steps and find a way.

In addition to these steps, a special focus on personalizing motivation by determining what players want to achieve goes a long way toward helping them today and in the future. The answer can vary from player to player, but there are some things that are common to most of them.

Some coaches believe that motivation takes care of itself no matter what you do. If someone wants to give it their all, they will. If they do not want to give it their all, they will not. Other coaches believe that motivation is as simple as a KITA approach: give them a kick in the as* and they will respond. That does not mean to really kick them, but these coaches tend to use a loud, aggressive, in-your-face approach as a motivation tool.

I believe there are times when motivation takes care of itself, but coaches may not be able to count on that. There are times when motivation needs some help, especially in team sports. Of course, there will be some stellar individuals and athletes who motivate themselves, but coaches need to motivate individuals and keep them motivated as part of a team. Coaches need to find out what their team wants collectively and then link individual goals and desires to that team desire. Follow a logical path to achieve the team desire, and you get motivation.

Coaches using the KITT approach must be careful. It is effective in a lot of situations but can be hard to sustain because it tends to deliver temporary cooperation. Motivation achieved this way can go away almost as soon as the player's ears stop ringing from your shouting. Then you need another in-your-face session to recreate the motivation. The more times you use this approach, the harder it is to duplicate your results. Now, there are times when this approach is extremely useful, but I think you must be winning championships for athletes and parents to put up with it over time. Since we know that not all coaches win championships, I doubt that you will get true motivation that is consistent over time by using it. I realize that many coaches win for many years using this approach. My only worry is how the player comes to deal with sports or life after going through this system. That is a subject for another time, another book. I just think the team may do well despite this approach, but there may not be a lot of fun around in this system of motivation.

I think that you need to find out what players want and cater to those wants if you are going to motivate them consistently. The simple answer is always that players want to win. That goes without saying. But search deeper into their desires. They want to be the best at their position. They want to go to the next level, maybe get a college scholarship. They want to be part of a team that everyone fears year in and year out. They want their contribution to the team to matter. They want the team to need them and they want to be involved when things get tough and the game is on the line. They want a season to remember, or a career to cherish. I think most importantly, players want to be respected, trusted, and supported. They want even-handed discipline. They want fair treatment, and they want to be rewarded for their efforts.

Those are a lot of wants, and you cannot to satisfy everyone. You can, however, set team goals that include many of the individual desires. Make sure everyone understands the team goals and how their individual desires can be satisfied through their support of the team. Get players to understand that they must be loyal to and respectful of the team's goals. Once you do this, motivation is no longer a one-way street. Everyone understands their commitment and should be 100 percent engaged in making team goals a reality. Now, you have linked the personal desires of your athletes to the team goal, so they should be motivated by the fact that they are working to accomplish things that are personally significant to them.

Any time your team gets bogged down and it seems they are straying from the path, revisit the relationship between individual and team goals to get back on course. Make everyone accountable for staying on course.

Motivating people also requires challenging them. Make them strive for things they have never achieved. Push them to work to a level of accomplishment they may not believe think they can reach. Striving for things greater than you imagine gets your adrenaline flowing.

Motivation requires allowing people to be creative. Early in my coaching career, I cringed when players did flashy things. For instance, I was worried when a basketball player passed the ball behind his back. I was uncomfortable when a football player left his assignment to make a big play like intercepting a pass. I was frustrated when a softball player tried to stretch her single into a double without a base coach signaling her on. But I learned along the way how much those things excite players. They let the player know you are willing to let them strive for greater achievements. I learned that no one ever made a big play without taking a risk. No one ever made news as the result of avoiding a risky move. Most of all, I learned that freelancing or thinking outside of the box is what makes playing sports exciting. Yes, now I savor creativity.

Why is the risk of creativity acceptable? I accept it because I am looking for all-out effort. I always tell my players that if they make a mistake, they better make sure they do it going full speed, full tilt. If you are going to take a risk, put all your effort into it. If you fail, work that much harder to make it right the next time. Players appreciate that kind of freedom, and they welcome the accountability that comes with it. This approach also allows players to test and identify their limits.

My approach does not always work the first time or the second time, but I always keep at it hoping to fix it before it adversely affects the search for success through motivation. Sometimes players avoid stretching themselves toward higher goals or stepping forward to greater challenges because they are afraid to fail. What do you do? I can tell you what I did several years back when I coached a youth league football team.

One of my players, Baconte, had difficulty getting himself to practice on time, had trouble working hard, and failed to follow instructions. One day, I was watching game films with some of my players. The players were trying to pressure this young man to work harder. They reminded him about the possibility of not playing much come game time. Then they said, "Isn't that right, coach?"

When I agreed, Baconte said, "Coach, that's okay. I don't need to play. All my friends are on the team, and they wear their game jerseys to school on Friday. I just want a game jersey so I can fit in."

I was shocked! I immediately wrote a check for the amount of his registration. I told him he needed to leave the team. I explained how it hurts a team to have members who are not fully engaged. Everyone should be all the way in or all the way out.

Baconte said he could not take the check to his father. He said he could not bear to leave the team, and he said he would do whatever was necessary to stay with us and become a better football player. I am not exactly sure how much of the change of heart came from my ultimatum, but I know it had an effect – just maybe not as much as his worry that he would not be able to explain to his father why he was no longer on the team.

Whatever the real reason for the change, the improvement was immediate and astounding. This young man dedicated himself that day and promised to do all he could to be a full, contributing member of the team.

He finished the season as one of our best players, and he had an outstanding effort in the championship game. He went on to be a starter on his high school football team on offense and defense.

The lesson in all of this is that coaches must find out what makes people do what they do. Everyone has a "hot button" for motivation; you just have to find it. In my example, I was determined to help this wonderful young man fully enjoy his first football experience. That determination forced me to find his "hot button."

Create Motivation Magnets

Another opportunity for coaches to motivate their team requires finding what I call a "Motivation Magnet." The Magnet is a player who inspires others to heightened effort and increased productivity. The Magnet is a trusted player who always gives straight answers regardless of what it means, positively or negatively, to their popularity.

Motivation Magnets save time for coaching staffs so they can take a break from motivation. When coaches are tending to other matters, trivial errors pop up and tend to demand more attention than they are worth in terms of substance, importance, and relationship to goal achievement. Magnets are wise athletes who are alert to how their efforts can save coaches time, and who will be on the lookout for ways they can help the coaching staff keep discipline at acceptable levels. Magnets are leaders working to ensure the team is successful. They will dare to be uniquely themselves in all situations, regardless of the pressure.

Not just anyone can be the Magnet. This is an individual who is loyal to the coach and the team, and who has the respect and admiration of their teammates. They do not play games at the expense of others, and they consistently fulfill their role. Most important, Magnets fully support the team effort when decisions are made, regardless of their position or personal feeling during deliberations. When they have gained a reputation for consistently doing all these things, they become Motivation Magnets.

Being a Magnet goes beyond these qualities because the person must be consistently present and attentive, efficient, and productive. They must have a great sense of self and be able to exhibit it to others without trying too hard.

Personalizing motivation, forcing unmotivated players to make choices, and finding Motivation Magnets are opportunities to help people see themselves in a brighter light and to create a personally rewarding environment. The difference can determine your team's success or failure in the long run through enhanced motivation.

Chapter 6

EI Can Help You

Figure 6. This is a way to leverage the thoughts, ideals, and motivations of your team to create success.

What is EI? Emotional Intelligence is the ability to sense, understand, and effectively apply the power and acumen of emotions as a source of human energy, information, trust, creativity, and influence[4]. EI helps leaders build a collaborative culture, emphasize every person's strengths including their own, and work to improve everyone's weaknesses. Smart leaders use EI to bond with their team and create open communication relationships that allow the same opportunities to a player who is new to the sport as they do to the team's best and brightest.

The benefits of EI are no secret, as explained in a 2018 examination of research on the subject. In that study, a group of researchers completed a 10-year examination of 44 studies on emotional intelligence in sports and found advantages to its use, aligning those benefits in four groups.

The findings suggest advantages for coaches and players in terms of performance, psychological skills, and factors that transcend sport. The groupings compared EI to psychological skills in sport, EI as it relates to coaching, EI as it relates to performance, and how and why EI can transcend sport.[5]

EI is said to have a net positive impact on sport-related variables as identified in 37 of 44 studies. The results showed that EI reduced the number of injuries in some athletes and had a positive effect on several psychological skills such as mental toughness, self-confidence, and precompetitive anxiety. All these items are contributors to player health and availability according to the study.

A major conclusion of the study's analysis is that those who cannot understand their own emotions and emotional experiences will not have an ability to help others control their own emotions. In other words, if coaches can reflect on their own emotions, the meaning of those emotions, and the underlying associations between emotions and outcomes, they can take meaningful steps to do the same for their players.

To use this information, coaches must understand that the fundamental cornerstones of EI are emotional literacy, emotional fitness, emotional depth, and emotional alchemy. Emotional literacy involves developing a clear and useful vocabulary to allow recognizing, respecting, and valuing the inherent wisdom of feelings. Emotional honesty, emotional energy, emotional feedback, and practical intuition contribute to emotional literacy.

Emotional fitness has trust as one of its key characteristics. Emotional fitness also includes authenticity, resilience, renewal, and constructive discontent. Trust is an actionable emotional strength – something we must feel and act on.

Emotional depth has to do with calling forth your core character, identifying and advancing the unique potential and purpose that define your destiny, manifesting commitment, drive, initiative, conscience, and accountability, applying integrity, and increasing your influence beyond authority, rank, and title.

Emotional alchemy is a blending of forces that enable us to discover creative opportunities and transform lesser ideas into greater ones.

Among these cornerstones, emotional literacy deserves a close examination. Emotional literacy is the ability to recognize, understand, and appropriately express our emotions. Just as verbal literacy is the basic building-block for reading and writing, emotional literacy is the basis for perceiving and communicating emotions. Becoming emotionally literate mean that coaches learn, or become aware of, the vocabulary or slang of each player as they work through their emotional lives.

A closer look reveals five key components in EI are self-awareness, self-regulation, social skill, empathy, and motivation. Self-awareness is the ability to know your emotions, strengths, and weaknesses. It is also the ability to understand what drives you and how your actions and reactions affect others. The benefits can include self-confidence, realistic self-assessment, ability to use humor, and acceptance of constructive criticism.

Self-regulation is the practice of managing your emotional state and to think before acting. What you do has consequences, and self-regulation is about looking before your leap. Self-regulation can foster trustworthiness, integrity, and comfort with change or ambiguity, all helpful characteristics when building your team.

Social skill is about a proficiency in managing relationships. You need to find common ground with your team and use that commonality to build rapport with everyone. Mastering social skills leads to effectiveness in leading change, persuasiveness, effective networking inside and outside of your team, and makes you better at building and leading teams.

The notion of networking inside your team may seem strange, but this is important. For example, one of your players has a good friend that does not play the sport but is an excellent athlete. Working with your player to meet that person and then getting to know them and their family is networking inside your team to improve networking outside of your team!

Empathy is the ability to understand and appreciate the emotions, needs, and concerns of others. Use empathetic concerns to guide your behavior. Sometimes, because of the crush of activity or the urgency of the game, you cannot do this, but it is important to consider it whenever you can. Use empathy to attract and retain talent. Your ability to see another person's point of view improves your ability to develop them and ensures that you are sensitive to cross-cultural differences.

Motivation is a passion and persistence that guides and facilitates reaching your goals. It can get you and the team moving when times are tough. It can convince people to try a difficult task when they do not believe they have to skill to accomplish it. Motivation gets everyone interested in accomplishing the task and addressing new challenges. It can create an unshakeable energy to improve and optimism when faced with failure. It is powerful!

No conversation about EI is complete without discussing trust. We trust people in the hopes that their behavior towards us will be satisfying and beneficial. Trust is hard to get and easy to lose. Once you lose someone's trust, you may never get it back. So, cherish this powerful tool.

Let people see who you really are and align your wants and desires with their wants and desires. This alignment strengthens your team in a trusting atmosphere.

EI is your access to all these things – self-awareness, self-regulation, social skill, empathy, motivation, trust – to help you. It allows you to do something we discussed in Chapter 1: *Look in The Mirror.* Use these skills to ensure your own improvement and bring a better you to your team. When you improve together, everyone is stronger.

Chapter 7

Self Preservation is Key

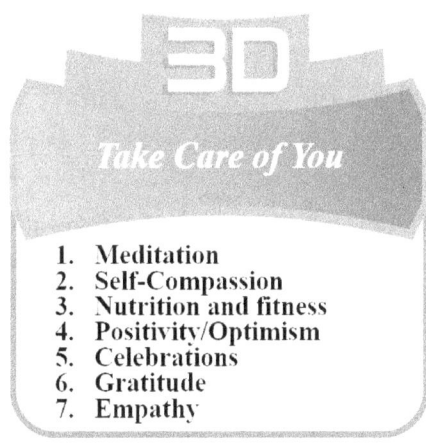

Figure 7. Nurture yourself through self-care that develops your psychological, spiritual, and virtue-based themes for overall health and wellness.

When we research sports, sports medicine, and health references, one of the things that we find is important to coaches and players is self-care. Let us focus on coaches because you must take care of yourself before you can take care of others. Self-care is about personal development of psychological, spiritual, and virtue-based themes that improve your overall health and alertness and free you to focus your full attention on your players when they need you.[6]

Taking care of your needs as they relate to your coaching ability is important. This is about finding ways to help yourself get the best of yourself. Your personal well-being can be improved by focusing on several variables, meditation, self-compassion, nutrition and fitness, positivity, optimism, celebrations, gratitude, and empathy.

This approach is based on the theory of self-compassion. The theory "...involves being touched by and open to one's own suffering, not avoiding or disconnecting from it, generating the desire to alleviate one's suffering and to heal oneself with kindness. Self-compassion also involves offering nonjudgmental understanding to one's pain, inadequacies, and failures, so that one's experience is seen as part of the larger human experience."[7]

While the self-compassion definition relates to addressing negative emotions or outcomes, this book suggests a proactive use of the theory. Being proactive means taking steps to look at yourself and to do the things that protect you from suffering from negativity. Avoiding negativity is important to improving yourself and helps you develop the skills you need to be effective when you engage with others. Taking a close look at the variables listed above can be used to guide you to a productive self-care approach.

Meditation is about slowing yourself down to reduce stress. Give yourself time to think so you can boost your physical, emotional, and mental health. Find a quiet spot without distractions and stay there for a set amount of time. Make yourself comfortable and focus on breathing naturally. Let your thoughts come naturally and focus on how you feel about them. Do not focus on solving anything, just experience this time alone. Make sure your daily schedule allows for rest and white space as much as you can. Listen to your mind and body and take a personal vacation when you need to.

Self-compassion requires that you find a way to personally affirm yourself. Now you can use that inner dialogue from meditation to drive you to quality performance, achievement, and, ultimately, motivation. Be supportive, compassionate, and kind to yourself and try to limit negative feeling and thinking. Self-compassion also suggests that you do all you can to avoid negative communications or to minimize their effects on you. Accept your emotions, good and bad, and adjust to them in the best way you can. Identify the things that trigger your emotions so you can develop effective responses to those emotions.

You already know that **nutrition and fitness** are connected in promoting your overall health. A review of health literature suggests that there are many factors involved in personal well-being. These can include physical exertion, being outdoors, stretching, exercise, nutrition, and even laughing. Work to be resilient, working and playing hard, recovering, and then doing it all over again. Find ways to replenish your energy and sharpen your focus.

Being **positive, optimistic**, and happy is a choice. Take time to do things you enjoy and share that with others. This applies to music, hobbies, TV, movies; whatever you like. Allow yourself large doses of positive emotions like forgiveness, optimism, gratitude, and commitment. All of these will make it easier to maintain your overall health.

Do not confine **celebrations** to the big victories. Small wins should be celebrated as well. If you increase your weightlifting limit, run an extra mile or two, achieve your weight loss goal, or just find an answer that you have been searching for, celebrate big! This personal shot in the arm can go a long way to thanking yourself for dedication, detail, and discipline.

As you take stock, be **grateful** for the family, friends, and opportunities you have. Share your grateful feelings with those around. Being humble is important too. This allows you to see and understand different perspectives in life and helps you see the source of the generosity or unearned privileges around you. It allows you to take life as it comes and to accept what happens in your environment.

Empathy is the way to understand another's perspective and to share the feelings experienced by someone else. Dealing with empathy while doing self-care can be challenging, and it may not be for everyone. Even if you do not address it for others, examine your inner empathy. Inner empathy is about understanding how you react to things and examining why and how those reactions affect your behaviors.

A good way to look at taking care of yourself is to meditate as often as you need to so you can focus on self-compassion. Practicing good nutrition and staying physically fit are contributors to a positive and optimistic outlook. Celebrating your small as well as big victories, being grateful for where you are and what you have and performing and leading with empathy will improve your leadership skills.

Chapter 8

The Total Coach

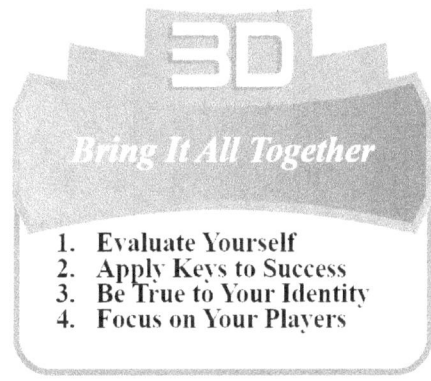

Figure 8. Use the results of self-examination and goal setting to apply your "new" identity with your players.

We are discussing what is necessary for you to be the total coach. To do that, be sure to self-evaluate and apply the keys you have identified that lead to your success. Be consistent in applying those keys and be true to your identity as a coach. This will lead you to the answer to an important question: "What's in it for me?"

If you are already providing many of the things I have mentioned in these pages, your task should be an easy one. Your task *should* be easy but be careful. You may be providing many things but keep striving for improvements and adjustments. Continue to get better.

If your self-assessment determines that you are falling short of providing for the "wants" that help keep your athletes motivated, you may need to do some improving and adjusting to show your players you care about their contributions. Finding ways to get players involved in improving and adjusting the process could be a great motivator. Help them see positive changes they can make in words and actions they own. The result will be buy-in and trust, not necessarily in that order.

Evaluate Yourself

Always evaluate yourself as a coach. We talked earlier about learning your craft in coaching clinics and using that knowledge to take a hard look at yourself and your program. Build on strengths and attack weaknesses.

Know what you want for your team and do what is necessary to get there based on the tools provided herein. Pursue a winning environment and be ready to adjust your strategy or restructure your approach to maintain it. Enjoy the ride. This profession can bring happiness and satisfaction beyond belief without necessarily requiring that you win championships. Make sure that you and your players have fun along the way.

Apply Keys to Success

The 3D principle I have introduced keeps you dedicated to the task at hand, ensures that you pay attention to all the details, and helps you establish the discipline your team needs to succeed. Dedication signals what we believe, forcing us to examine ourselves and our fundamentals. Dedication keeps us tied to our values.

Attention to detail makes sure that we hone our skills and perfect our craft. We learn new things as our skills improve and we keep working even if we are satisfied with today's outcomes.

We discussed supportive discipline that helps us work together with our players to see their potential and develop it. Discipline gives consistency and order to our program and can create a comfort zone where there is a shared understanding of what is expected of each member of the team.

Be careful to correct problems in a positive direction. If people are behaving in the wrong way or moving in the wrong direction, your correction should get them started on the right track and then let them work toward consistency. If your correction motivates them to speed up and they are going in the wrong direction, they will just get lost faster. If your correction makes them too cautious to act, the right time to act on the issue might pass them by. Find balance in your approach.

Finally, help people see what your sport is all about. Help them understand that they are judged by the quality of each hour they spend with you. Let them know that their efforts tie directly to the benefits they will derive from participation. Motivated people decide what they want and then work on getting what they want. They may have to do some things along the way that do not show a direct relationship to the goal, but they keep moving on the path anyway. They apply 100 percent effort to whatever they are doing now as they build a reputation for success.

Be True to Your Identity

As you verify the reasons why you coach and understand your goals, you will improve your coaching ability. I guarantee it. Ask these questions on a regular basis, or at least before each season begins, and you will have a fresh focus on your efforts and outcomes.

The vision you identify will guide you in success and in tough times. Ultimately, these high and low points will deliver many exciting rewards and experiences. Match this understanding with how you develop your players, and your coaching will stand the test of time. You will handle all the personalities of players, parents, and administrators and you will build character that shows itself year in and year out.

Focus on Your Players

When I think about coaching my late daughter Antoinette, and about some of the great players I have encountered like Steve, Alison, Baconte, Nick, Brent, Chris, and Lisa, to name a few, I focus on player interaction. Your success depends on energizing people to give the effort and enthusiastically put the team above themselves to win. Your vision helps the players to be ready, willing, and able to put even grievances aside when they understand the path you have chosen for them. This is when you know you have created an effective team.

Successful people are confident and competent, and they find ways to be productive. Your motivation efforts help to find out what drives your players. Successful people in organizations ensure they do what it takes to satisfy the mission. Successful organizations provide the resources and professional atmosphere that allow their members to do what they do best. If you highlight them, understand them, praise them, equip them, focus them, train them, join with them, and cherish them, you will find success. Who knows how long it will take, but I fully believe you will be on your way to achieving success.

Challenging people is important to motivating them. You want them to strive for something more than they think might be possible. You want to allow them to be creative in that pursuit, because that allows them to think outside the box. They may perform better than ever with this kind of freedom.

There are some fundamental needs of players that coaches should keep in mind. They involve making athletes earn playing time, allowing them to participate, showing them how to be graceful, helping them mature, granting them your personal time, letting them have fun, and allowing their parents to be part of the team.

Be sure to develop character. Look at the life each player is living. Are you helping? Are you allowing the sport to be something other than number one in his or her life? Help them see that this is an enhancement to their life, not the primary reason for living.

Character stays with you even when your talent fails you. Character never goes in a slump unless you let it. Character exercises and improves skills in the off season. Character is always present, while effort sometimes takes a play or a day off. When you have tough choices to make, character leads the way.

See why character is so important? Teams and coaches seek two kinds of players. First, talented athletes who make the money plays. Second, athletes with character who hold the team together and provide the little things that are not always recognized. Here are some examples of character:

- A player stays behind to pick up equipment when it is not his or her turn.
- A player intervenes at a party to steer others away from a bad situation.
- Someone organizes a player's only meeting during a losing streak.

- A player comforts another player who just made a big mistake that cost the team the game.
- A player is the first to visit an injured player in the hospital right after the game.

These examples illustrate why players with talent *and* character are so easy to admire and follow. Players like basketball great Michael Jordan, football great Peyton Manning, the late boxer Muhammad Ali, hockey great Wayne Gretzky, tennis stars Chris Evert, Martina Navratilova and Serena Williams, and baseball greats Johnny Bench, Hank Aaron, and Cal Ripken Jr. to name a few. They were, and are, bigger than their sport and bigger than life, but not just because of their talent. They all possessed outstanding character.

My keys to focusing on your players are:

- Let them play
- Let them compete
- Help them win and lose gracefully
- Always demonstrate coaching professionalism and maturity
- Let them have your personal time and attention when they ask
- Give them your personal time and attention when they have a crisis, even if they do not ask
- Let them have fun
- Let their parents and extended families participate in a way that does not detract from learning the game

Above all, be a coach they can look to for help, advice, guidance, and sometimes even a gentle push in the right direction. This is not easy, and some coaches struggle with the difficulties involved in motivating people.

Do not panic. Set the example and be ready for action when your team needs you most. Be patient and always remember that you cannot make them follow you, but you can convince them to participate. The commitment you demonstrate as their coach will solidify the team's direction and entice everyone to participate in the right way.

References

1. Retrieved November 23, 2020, from N.C. State University, https://faculty.chass.ncsu.edu/slatta/hi216/learning/why_self_assess.htm.
2. Retrieved November 21, 2020, from http://www.espn.com/page2/s/list/topupsets/010525.html.
3. Retrieved November 22, 2020, from Inc.com, https://www.inc.com/marcel-schwantes/8-powerful-ways-to-motivate-inspire-your-employees-this-week.html.
4. Cooper, R. K. (1997). Applying emotional intelligence in the workplace. Training & development, 51(12), 31-39.
5. Magrum, E. D., Waller, S., Campbell, S., & Schempp, P. G. (2019). Emotional intelligence in sport: A ten-year review (2008-2018). *International Journal of Coaching Science, 13*(2), 3-32.
6. Devenish-Meares, P. (2015). Call to Compassionate Self-Care: Introducing Self-Compassion Into the Workplace Treatment Process. *Journal of spirituality in mental health, 17*(1), 75-87. doi:10.1080/19349637.2015.98557.
7. Neff, K. (2003). Self-Compassion: An Alternative Conceptualization of a Healthy Attitude Toward Oneself. *Self & Identity, 2*(2), 85. doi:10.1080/15298860309032.

Michael A. "Doc" Brown, Sr., Ph.D. has authored several books and is an accomplished public speaker. He has coached different sports at the recreation league, middle school, junior varsity, high school, and adult levels. He earned his Public Administration and Urban Policy degree, International Business, from Old Dominion University (ODU) in May 2011. He is teaching online social media, public relations, and communication courses for Florida Institute of Technology. He is a Navy civil servant working as a public affairs officer in Norfolk, Virginia. This PR professional has 40-plus years of military and civilian experience combined. He is an Air Force retiree who served 24 years in uniform.

www.ingramcontent.com/pod-product-compliance
Lightning Source LLC
Chambersburg PA
CBHW062146100526
44589CB00014B/1700